Growing up in ROMAN BRITAIN

Frances Wilkins

B.T. Batsford Ltd *London*

© Frances Wilkins 1979
First published 1979

ISBN 0 7134 0773 5

Printed by The Anchor Press Ltd, Tiptree, Essex
for the Publishers B T Batsford Limited
4 Fitzhardinge Street, London W1H 0AH

Frontispiece: **Girl with Kitten**

Acknowledgment

The Author and Publishers thank the following for their kind permission to reproduce copyright illustrations: The Bodley Head for fig 41 (from J. Balsdon, *Life and Leisure in Ancient Rome*, 1969); The Trustees of the British Museum for fig 4; City Museum and Art Gallery, Gloucester for fig 3; Corinium Museum, Cirencester for figs 7 and 61; Department of the Environment (Crown Copyright — reproduced with permission of the Controller of Her Majesty's Stationery Office) for fig 53; Pat Hodgson Library for figs 9, 14, 16, 21, 24, 26, 30, 45 and 47; Italian State Tourist Office (Foto-Enit-Roma) for fig 27; Mansell Collection for the jacket illustration and figs 11, 13, 19, 23, 33, 36, 42 and 44; Musée d'Aquitaine for fig 56; the Museum of London for figs 2, 20, 34, 35, 38, 40, 51 and 52; Photo Ellebé for fig 43; M. and C.H.B. Quennell for fig 46; Radio Times Hulton Picture Library for figs 1, 5, 6, 8, 12, 17, 18, 22, 23, 28, 32, 37, 39, 48, 49, 55, 60 and 64; the Warburg Institute for figs 10, 15, 29, 50, 54, 58 and 63. Thanks also are expressed to Pat Hodgson for the picture research on this book.

Contents

Acknowledgment 2
List of Illustrations 4

1 Roman Britain 5
2 Education 11
3 Girls 18
4 Growing up in a Town 24
5 Growing up in a Villa 30
6 Food 36
7 Clothes 43
8 Religion 48
9 Games and Pastimes 55
10 Poor Children 60

Table of Major Events 65
Glossary 67
A Selection of Sites in Roman Britain 68
Places to Visit 69
Books for Further Reading 70
Index 71

The Illustrations

1 The Romans land at Kent
2 A Roman palace in London
3 Romano-British head
4 Coins of Roman Britain
5 Saxons invade British coast
6 The Romans leave Britain
7 Mosaic craftsman's workshop
8 Schoolboy's wax tablet
9 Writing materials
10 Family tombstone, showing Roman numerals
11 A pupil and his schoolmasters
12 Minerva, goddess of school-children
13 Mother, father and baby
14 A lyre
15 A single tibia
16 Slaves with a Roman lady
17 Family altar in wealthy home
18 Roman betrothal ring
19 Wedding scene
20 Defensive wall
21 Roman vehicles
22 A Roman shop
23 A cutler's shop
24 Scene from a Roman comedy
25 Gladiators
26 Roman villa (plan)
27 The verandah of a Roman villa
28 Interior of a Roman villa
29 Floor mosaic
30 Remains of a hypocaust
31 Family chest
32 A Roman chair
33 Tenant farmers pay tribute
34 A market in the forum
35 Roman officer supervises shipment of food
36 Greengrocer's shop
37 A pork butcher and his wife
38 A Roman kitchen
39 Cooking implements
40 At a Roman meal
41 Musicians
42 Shopkeepers examine cloth
43 Tunics
44 A cloth-merchant's shop
45 Roman footwear
46 Fullers
47 An Arch-druid
48 The Temple of Diana at Ephesus
49 A sacrifice to the Lares
50 Mercury
51 Mithras
52 Ceremony in temple to Mithras
53 Remains of a Roman temple
54 A Roman priest
55 A Christian schoolmaster beaten to death
56 Young girl with pets
57 Hare-hunting
58 Dog
59 Wrestlers
60 A charioteer
61 A board game
62 A Roman village
63 Child's coffin
64 A Roman farm
65 Agricultural scenes in mosaic

1 Roman Britain

The Romans first came to Britain in 55 BC. They were led by Julius Caesar, who had recently conquered Gaul (the Roman name for France). In fact, one of the reasons for the Roman invasion of Britain was that a powerful tribe called the Belgae, who lived in the south of England, were inciting the Gauls, with whom they traded, to rebel and to try to drive the Romans out of France. There was another equally important reason for the invasion, though: the Romans coveted all the valuable natural resources in Britain. They had heard that there were not only fields of waving corn but also rich deposits of tin, copper and lead, and perhaps even of silver and gold.

Caesar's first expedition to Britain was not a success, however. He lost many of his supply ships in a storm, and also underestimated the strength of the British resistance. He left after only four or five days, but he had seen enough to realize that it would be well worth returning to this country as soon as the opportunity arose. He did come back to Britain less than a year later, bringing nearly three times as many men as before and far more supplies and equipment. Indeed, it seemed as if the Romans would quickly overrun the whole country, but before they could make any real progress, Caesar had to leave to put down further uprisings in Gaul.

For the next hundred years the Romans were busy elsewhere. However, they did not forget Britain. Various emperors and generals planned to make the country part of the Roman Empire, but it was not until 43 AD that (again because of trouble in Gaul) the Emperor Claudius finally gave orders that Britain was to be conquered.

This time the campaign went exactly according to plan. Within a matter of weeks all the tribes in the south and the midlands had been subdued. Their territory was then either directly annexed by the Romans or else entrusted to friendly local chiefs to be ruled as protectorates. The rest of the country was less easy to conquer. The fierce resistance of some of the northern tribes led to more than thirty years of intermittent warfare. However, the conquest was finally completed in about 80 AD. by an extremely able Roman general named Julius Agricola.

From that time onwards Britain was officially a Roman Province. This meant that it was administered by various officials under the direct supervision of the Emperor from Rome. In practice, though, even after the fighting had come to an end, the north and west of the country had not been effectively subdued. Because they could not be controlled by any civil authority, these regions remained occupied military zones throughout the whole of the Roman period. They were covered with forts and a network of strategic roads to connect them, and were practically devoid of any peaceful, civilized life.

In the south, the east and the midlands the situation was different. The people there quickly began to appreciate the advantages of the Roman way of life. They were soon inter-marrying with the

Roman settlers, and happily adopting not only their language but also their customs, culture and religion. When people talk about Roman Britain they usually mean this settled area. In fact, the south, the east and the midlands are the only part of the country where a Romano-British way of life can really be said to have existed. Therefore, this book about the way in which children in Roman Britain were brought up, educated,

1 The Romans land at Kent

2 A Roman palace in London, Cannon Street. The British adopted Roman building styles

fed and clothed and about how they amused themselves can deal only with this peaceful, Romanized part of the country.

Roman Britain reached its zenith in the fourth century AD, under the Emperor Constantine. Its population had increased enormously under Roman rule, and trade and industry were both flourishing. The country was by that time being raided by Saxon pirates, however, and the Romans had been compelled to fortify and garrison most of the east and south-east coast. As long as the Romans remained in Britain the pirates were always driven off, but towards

◄ 3 Head of a Romano-British man

4 Coins of Roman Britain: 1 shows the head of Emperor Claudius; 2 shows the head of Emperor Hadrian

5 Saxons invade the British coast

6 The Romans leave Britain

the end of the fourth century AD the Romans began to have troubles at home. Italy itself was being attacked by hordes of fierce barbarians, and the Romans had no alternative but to withdraw their troops from Britain to defend their own country. The chief citizens of Britain appealed to the Romans to send reinforcements to help defend them against the Saxons. No doubt the Romans intended to do so, but they had to drive the barbarians out of Italy first. A few years later the Britons appealed to them again, but by this time Rome itself was on the point of collapse, and there was nothing the Romans could do to help their former Province.

Once the Romans had left Britain, the Saxon raids became more and more frequent. What was more, the Saxons often decided not to return home after a raid, but to settle down in Britain. As a result, the Roman influence in Britain steadily declined, and within a hundred or so years it had almost completely disappeared.

When we think of Roman Britain there is one very important fact to remember: how long the Roman occupation of the country endured. From the time of the Romans' arrival in Britain (43 AD) to the disappearance of the last traces of Roman administration (about 429 AD) was nearly four hundred years. To understand how long this was, imagine that, if the Romans had arrived in Britain towards the end of the Tudor period, they would still be in occupation of the country today. This book is therefore dealing with a very considerable period of Britain's history, although it took place so long ago, and with many generations of children.

2 Education

Education under the Roman system was divided into three stages. The first two correspond roughly to modern primary and secondary schools, and the third to universities. Education was not compulsory in Roman Britain, however, and for various reasons the great majority of children attended only the first, or elementary stage, and many of them never went to school at all.

In early Roman times a shortage of schools made it difficult for many children to receive schooling. Unless children lived in a city or in one of the larger towns there was usually no school within reach. However, some of the later emperors, in particular Hadrian (see picture 4), were keen that schools should be opened everywhere, and they even gave special tax relief to teachers who would set up schools in remote places.

Another difficulty was that education was not free. Therefore, most of the poorer children, whose parents could not pay, generally had no opportunity of attending school. Also, many families considered that only boys needed to be educated, and so a great number of girls were never sent to school, and those who were usually attended only the first or elementary stage.

Elementary schools

The average elementary school had only ten to twelve children. This meant that the fees paid by the parents did not usually add up to enough to provide the teacher with a living. As a result, many teachers had other jobs as well, such as running a small workshop, which they did once the children had gone home in the afternoon.

It was the teacher's responsibility to find some accommodation for his pupils. Some classes were taught in a corner of the teacher's workroom or even under an awning fixed up outside his shop, so that they were in the middle of constant hustle and bustle, or surrounded by all the noises and disturbances of the town. There was very little furniture in the classroom. The master sat on a hard, upright chair, while the children sat on benches and balanced their writing tablets on their knees. (Every child had to provide his own wax tablet and a stylus, with which he scratched on the wax, his own pen and ink, his papyrus rolls and his abacus.)

The syllabus in the elementary schools was extremely narrow. The teachers concentrated almost entirely on teaching the children to read and write. This must have been quite difficult for some early Romano-British children to learn, though, as all the teaching was in Latin, and many of them spoke only Celtic at home. The only other subject taught was some simple arithmetic. Again, this must have been made less easy by the very cumbersome method the Romans used for writing their figures. Even addition and subtraction must have been quite complicated, for example, when 88 was written LXXXVIII.

The children stayed at elementary school until they were about twelve years old. Then, if they were lucky, they went on for a further three or four years to one of the

◄ 7 The workshop of a mosaic craftsman. A school class might have taken place in a workshop like this

8 A schoolboy's wax tablet

9 Writing materials: a round box of papyrus rolls, pens, ink bottles, etc.

D M FLAVIAE AVGVSTINAE
VXIT A XXXVIIII M VII D XI FILIVS
SAENVS AVGSTINVS V X T A I D III
R V X T A I M VIII D V C AERESIVS
IN VS VET LEG VI VIC CONIVCI CARI
SS F ET SIBI F C

◀ 10 Complicated Roman numerals can be seen in the inscription of this family tombstone

grammar, or secondary, schools. Like the elementary schools, these were usually one-teacher schools, but the master was generally much better educated than the elementary school teacher, and had quite often studied in Greece.

Secondary schools

The secondary stage of education was mainly concerned with grammar and literature. The boys studied not only the great Roman writers but also the Greek writers in their original tongue. Other subjects taught included history, geography and sometimes philosophy. Occasionally the boys also learnt geometry, but little else was taught in the way of mathematics or science. Music was rarely, if ever, taught to better-off boys. Playing an instrument or singing was regarded only as a fit occupation for slaves. Boys learnt poetry, however, and this was sometimes set to music and sung, generally to an accompaniment played on a lyre by a slave.

11 A pupil apologises to his schoolmasters for being late

Final education

After leaving the grammar school, the wealthy Romano-British boys began the final stage of their education. This was the study of public speaking. For it was presumed that all educated Romans would be constantly speaking and debating on various councils and in the courts. The boys had to learn how to find and arrange suitable subject matter, how to speak clearly in public, and how to present their arguments when they took part in debates. This final stage of a boy's education usually lasted three or four years, but boys could go on studying as long as they were interested, and their parents could afford to pay the fees. Most parents considered public speaking extremely important, as they believed that it would help their sons to have successful careers, either in the law courts or in some form of government service.

School life

In all the stages of education the school year began in March. This was at the end of the annual holiday of Minerva, the special goddess of school-children. There were no weekends, as we know them, but every ninth day was a holiday. There were also numerous religious feast-days throughout

the year, when all the schools were closed.

The school day lasted six hours in every type of school. Lessons began at dawn and broke off around midday, when the children either went home for their lunch or ate the picnic they had brought with them. There was then another hour or two of lessons in the afternoon. School was over well before dusk, even during the dark days of winter.

The time spent at school must have seemed endless to most of the children, though, as everything was taught by continuous repetition. In the elementary schools the children spent hours copying down proverbs over and over again, and when they were older they had to learn countless long passages of literature by heart.

The discipline was harsh in all schools in Roman Britain. To receive two or three strokes of the cane on the hand for laziness or inattention was a part of everyday life for most children. For serious misdemeanours the older boys were even flogged: two other pupils held the boy still while the master beat him with a long leather whip.

12 Statue of Minerva, the special goddess of school-children

3 Girls

In early times all Romano-British families wanted sons. This was because boys could help to cultivate the land or follow their fathers in a trade. Indeed, poorer people sometimes left their daughters to die, and even quite rich families considered it a tragedy if more than one daughter was born. However, people's ideas gradually changed. As they became steadily more prosperous and secure they felt less need for sons who could work for their living. In addition, with the coming of Christianity people began to believe in the sanctity of all human life, and girls eventually came to be valued just as much as their brothers.

13 Mother, father and baby

Consecration

When baby girls were eight days old a special religious ceremony was held. (A similar ceremony was held for baby boys, but not until they were nine days old.) The ceremony might take place either at home or in the temple, and the purpose was to consecrate the child's life to the gods. During the ceremony a lucky charm was hung around the baby's neck. This was supposed to ward off all evil influences until the child was grown up. The charm, which was either round or heart-shaped, was made of gold if the family was rich, but otherwise it was usually made of leather.

Girls' education

Only a small number of girls ever went to school. Those who did were mostly the better-off, and they were usually escorted there and back by a nursemaid. Generally, they started school at the age of seven or eight, and left as soon as they could read and write reasonably well, which was usually at about the age of eleven.

Better-off girls continued their education at home with a tutor, however. Here they studied chiefly Greek and Roman literature, both in their original tongues. They also learnt to dance, to sing and to play the lyre, and to do the beautiful embroidery for which Romano-British women were famous.

A girl's most important lessons were learnt from her mother. These were how to cook, spin and weave, and in general how to look after a family. In the case of wealthy girls, it was also important to learn how to

14 A girl playing a square lyre

15 A girl with a single tibia, a wind instrument ▶

direct slaves, for they might one day have several dozen under their immediate control.

Marriage

When a girl was 14 she was considered ready for marriage. The age was the same both for well-to-do girls and for girls from poorer families. In both cases the marriage was usually arranged by the girl's father. Girls themselves had little or no choice in the matter of whom they married.

The evening before the wedding a special religious ceremony took place, at which the girl placed all her toys and her outgrown clothes on the altar of the household gods, the Lares (see page 50). She also laid her lucky charm on the altar, as once she was married she would have a husband to protect her and would no longer need the charm.

The next morning was a very busy one for the bride. If she was rich, her slaves

fussed around her for several hours with all her cosmetics: chalk to whiten her neck and forehead, red ochre to put on her lips and cheeks, and either powdered antimony or ashes to darken her eyebrows. The slaves then used hot tongs to put some curls in her hair. (Girls in Roman Britain always let their hair grow long and parted it in the middle.) If the bride was very fashion-conscious she might even have some artificial curls and ringlets attached to her own hair to make a frame round her face.

◄ 16   Slaves attend to the hair and jewellery of a Roman lady in this drawing by a Victorian artist

Last of all the bride dressed in a long, white woollen tunic. By tradition this had no hem and was tied at the waist with a special double knot in the woollen girdle. She also put a bright yellow cloak round her shoulders, bright yellow sandals on her feet, and covered her head and face with a transparent, flame-coloured veil.

17   The family altar is on the left of this picture of a wealthy Roman home

The time and the date of the wedding depended on the priest saying that all the omens for that moment were good. The wedding ceremony itself took place in front of the family altar. As well as the priest, there had to be ten witnesses present (five from the bride's family and five from the groom's). The young couple clasped their right hands together and solemnly exchanged their vows of life-long faithfulness.

If a free-born girl did not get married, there was hardly anything she could do instead. Usually, she had to go to live with a married sister or brother. There were a few women shopkeepers, teachers and doctors, but in general all jobs of this kind were undertaken by slaves.

Going out

When better-off girls went out they often travelled in a kind of light gig. This had two wheels, and was pulled usually by a pair of ponies. The gig held three people, sitting side by side, but it had no cover, and so if it was raining, a girl had to put up her umbrella. Really rich girls, on the other hand, often went out in a litter. This was a kind of covered chair with a long wooden handle at each corner. The handles were

18 A Roman betrothal ring, showing right hands clasped together

19 A wedding scene

held by four slaves, who had been specially bought to make a team, all being of similar stature, so that they could carry the litter on their shoulders without tilting it.

Well-born girls did not often go out at night before they were married. There was no street-lighting, and there were often robbers and cut-throats about. Even adults, if they went out after dark, usually took a couple of armed slaves with them to carry torches in front of them and to defend them if necessary.

4 Growing up in a Town

The town plan
The towns in Roman Britain were all built on the same plan. They were roughly square or rectangular and surrounded by a high defensive wall. All the streets were straight and criss-crossed each other at right angles, including the two main thoroughfares, which led out of the town through four heavily fortified gates.

In the centre of the town there was an open space called a forum. This was used mainly as a market place (see picture 34), although all kinds of public gatherings, such as political and religious meetings, took place there at times. On one side of the forum stood the basilica, which was rather like a town hall and law courts combined, and on the other three sides there were rows of small shops. Some of the shops were just tiny lock-ups (see picture 7), but others had been converted from the front room of the house where the shopkeeper and his family lived. Both sorts of shop were wide open to the street all day, but heavily shuttered at night, as there was no adequate police force to patrol the streets after dark.

20 Part of the defensive wall round London

21 Roman vehicles on one of the roads out of the town. You can see the fortified gate in the wall in the background

Running off from every side of the forum were streets of houses. Romano-British houses were nearly all long and narrow, with one of their narrow ends facing the street. There were no indoor corridors, but the homes of the better-off people usually had a long, covered verandah which led from one room to another (see picture 27). There were no names on the streets or numbers on the houses, but as there was no postal service there were at least no postmen to be worried about this! There were carters, though, who (to add to their difficulties) were not allowed to deliver their goods

22 A Roman shop opening onto the street

until after dark, because of the traffic jams in the towns during the day.

The town-dwellers

Most of the well-to-do town-dwellers were lawyers of one kind or another. The Romans had an enormous respect for the law and for the legal profession in general. Almost everyone in public life, from the governors of the towns downwards, had received some legal training, and had usually started their career in the courts. The rest of the town-dwellers were mostly craftsmen and artisans: carpenters, tanners, weavers, potters and so on. Most of them owned small one-man businesses, and their workrooms were usually also shops where they could sell what they made (see pictures 7 and 23).

Life for the lawyers' children was obviously different from life for the craftsmen's children. For example, the better-off children were always sent to the best schools available. They also quite often had a personal slave (usually a Greek) who would give them individual tuition in any subjects which they did not happen to be able to study at school. In addition, since the wealthy town-dweller often owned some land just outside the city wall, the well-to-do children had the opportunity to learn how to manage an estate. The artisans' sons, on the other hand, left school as soon as they had finished their elementary education, and immediately began helping their fathers in the workshop.

23 A Roman cutler in his shop

Feasts and festivals

Nevertheless, some aspects of life were the same for rich and poor. For instance, all the children joined in the religious celebrations in the towns. The Romano-British year was studded with feasts and festivals of various gods, when everyone met outside the temples, and the priests addressed them or led them in prayer. At the major festivals there were also processions through the towns. These were usually very exciting affairs, and everyone, including the children, joined in. The processions included bands, which were made up of wind instruments mostly, particularly trumpets of all kinds, as well as cymbals, drums and tambourines.

Entertainment

Children of all classes went to the theatre. Plays and pageants were performed quite regularly in most towns, especially on festival days. They sometimes took place in the forum, but the bigger towns had a special round or oval open-air arena, surrounded by rows of wooden or stone benches. These arenas were also used for gladiator fights from time to time, but fighting to the death, either between two men or between a man and an animal, hardly ever took place in Roman Britain. Cock-fighting and bear-baiting were quite commonplace, though, and if the arena was large enough there were sometimes also chariot races.

The public baths

The place where children most often met, though, was undoubtedly the public baths,

◄ 24   A scene from a Roman comedy

25   Gladiators

easily the most popular social centre in every town. Fortunately, the admission fee was low, so that almost everyone could afford to visit the baths, although only the better-off people could pay for some of the expensive extras, such as the services of a masseur.

The Roman public baths can be compared not only to the baths we have in our homes today but also, in many ways, to present-day Turkish baths. The aim was not only to get clean, but also to tone up the whole body, and at the same time to spend a pleasant hour or two in company with other people of the town.

Firstly everyone, adults and children, went into a special room to undress. Then they entered the first of a series of four or five rooms with special underfloor heating. Each room they visited was hotter than the one before, until at last they reached a room which was so hot that they all began to pour with sweat. After spending a short time in this room they massaged themselves with olive oil supplied by the baths. Then they scraped themselves all over with a strigil, which they got from a bath attendant. This was an instrument, rather like a small blunt sickle, to remove dead skin. In the last room there was a large cold bath. Here, after jumping in and perhaps swimming around for a few strokes, the bathers climbed out and had a brisk towelling.

After drying themselves, people put on a loin-cloth or a loose wrap and either sat and talked at the edge of the pool or perhaps played a game together. Some of the bigger baths had not only a special area for games and exercises, but even such facilities as a restaurant or a library.

5 Growing up in a Villa

Not all Romano-British families lived in the towns. Some of the most wealthy had large country houses, called villas, surrounded by extensive estates. In fact, by the fourth century AD there were at least six or seven hundred of these villas, dotted around all over the country, some of them covering as much area as two present-day football pitches.

26 Plan of a Roman villa

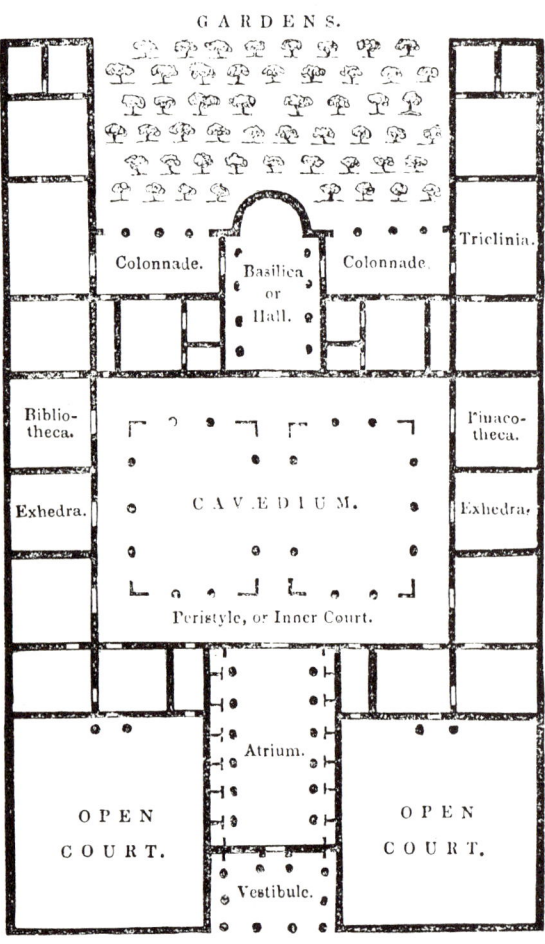

The building and site of the villa

Originally a villa was a long, narrow, rectangular building. It was usually all on one floor, although cellars and attics were not entirely unknown. As time went on, however, villas came to be built with one or even two wings at the sides, and eventually many villas formed three, or even four, sides of a square. The lower part of the outside walls was constructed of stone, covered with stucco, but the upper part, in most areas of the country, was made of wattle and daub. The roofs of the villas were generally made of curly red tiles, but the roofs of the outbuildings, such as stables and barns, were usually of thatched reeds or straw.

It must have been pleasant for a child to grow up in a villa. For a start, the villas were always sited in the most attractive position available, often on the side of a south-facing slope. This meant that they caught whatever sunshine there was, and in most cases also had a beautiful view over the surrounding countryside. In addition, the villas always had large gardens. These were generally laid out rather formally, but there was plenty of space where the children could play. And furthermore, a villa always had a long, covered verandah to join the various rooms (there were no corridors) and the children could play here in the fresh air even when it was not warm enough to play out of doors.

27 The covered verandah connecting the rooms ▶ of a Roman villa. The children could play here

Inside the villa

The villas were gay and attractive inside. The rooms were small, but the walls were usually plastered with brightly coloured pictures of birds, animals and flowers. The floors were covered with gay patterns or pictures (such as scenes from ancient myths), made out of tiny pieces of coloured marble, inlaid in a ground of stucco. This inlaid work was called mosaic.

From the third century onwards the villas were well heated. Even in winter the temperature in the principle rooms was always kept at about 20° centigrade by underfloor heating (or hypocausts). The floors were raised on small pillars and hot air from a large furnace was made to circulate in the space between the floor and the ground. The furnace was kept alight with wood and charcoal. (In some parts of the country there was coal, but it was used only in the areas where it was found.) The furnace also heated the water for the villa's bathrooms. There was usually one tepid, one hot and one cold bath, as in the public baths in the town.

Most of the water used in the villa came from a nearby stream or spring, but rainwater was also collected from the roof and the courtyard, especially for flushing the toilets. In most villas the toilets were somewhere near the baths, and consisted of a long row of wooden seats, with a communal gutter running along underneath them.

Furniture

There was very little furniture in the average villa. Even the main rooms often contained only a few folding stools, and some cushions scattered around on the floor. Many families had a large chest with a lock, however, in which they kept their most valued possessions, and sometimes there were some cupboards attached to the walls.

28 Brightly decorated walls and floor in a villa

29 Floor mosaic showing the wolf and the twins, Romulus and Remus

In the dining room there was a low table surrounded by couches. The men of the family always reclined at full length while they were having their meals (see picture 40). The women and children were generally allowed to sit on stools or low chairs with arms but no backs, and to place their food on a small occasional table.

Most of the kitchen was occupied by a huge square stove. This had several little hollows scooped out on top; charcoal and dry tinder were placed in each of the hollows, and the tinder was set alight with a spark struck from a piece of flint on some stone. The cooks then fried or boiled the food over the heat.

▲
30 Remains of an underfloor furnace, or hypocaust

31 Chest with a lock for the family's valuable possessions
▼

33 Tenant farmers pay tribute to the villa-owner

There was sometimes a little more furniture in the bedrooms. This included several large chests for clothes, as well as a number of cupboards and shelves. In the children's rooms there were also stools, so that the children could climb into bed. Although the beds were only like couches, they were nearly always very high off the ground.

From the third century onwards there was glass in the windows, and for the first time people could keep out of the cold and yet let in the light. The only artificial light was provided by candles or oil-lamps, but these were so smoky and smelly that most families avoided using them and went to bed almost as soon as it became dark.

Slaves' quarters

One wing of the villa was always used as the slaves' quarters. It had its own entrance and had no direct link with the rest of the house. Sometimes as many as two hundred slaves lived in this special wing, although most of them were not employed in the villa itself, but just on the estate.

The estate

The estate in most cases consisted mainly of farm-land. Most villa-owners gained their income almost entirely from agriculture. They usually worked a certain amount of their estate themselves, and let out the rest to tenant farmers, who paid them either in cash or in kind. Other villa-owners had one or more small industries on their estates: maybe a tannery, pottery, tile-works or brickworks or even a mine. Indeed, some villas were specially sited in an area because there was clay there or because coal or some other important mineral had been found on the land.

32 A Roman chair

6 Food

Buying the food

Not everyone in Roman Britain went to the shops for food. The majority of people who lived in the country produced nearly everything they needed themselves. Most of the townspeople, however, bought their food at the shops and markets, and many rich people who lived in the country visited the towns when they wanted to buy a special delicacy.

In almost every town the market was held in the forum. Most of the stalls belonged to the local farmers, most of whom came into the town to sell their produce themselves. On the other hand, some stalls were set up by merchants and traders, who had brought the goods which they were selling from other parts of the country, or even from quite distant parts of the Roman Empire.

Most permanent shops were clustered around the forum. They all opened directly on to the street, but there was often a counter across the front of a shop. If the shopkeeper sold the kind of goods which had to be weighed, he had a steel yard-arm on the counter, a balance with a pan hanging from one end and a moveable weight on the arm at the top (see picture 37).

Roman shopkeepers did not deliver their goods to customers, and so better-off Romano-British housewives usually sent their slaves to the shops for them. However, if they wanted some special luxuries, such as food from abroad, they would go to the shops or market themselves, sometimes taking their children with them. It must have been fascinating for the children to see all the different kinds of food on sale. At the greengrocer's, for example, there were not only the locally grown fruits, but many less common types from abroad. Apples, pears, cherries, plums and blackberries were all popular, but so (among the better-off people, at least) were oranges, figs, dates and olives. Certain fruits and vegetables were completely unknown in Roman times, however. These included potatoes, bananas and pineapples, which did not grow in any part of the known world at that time. Fruit and vegetables were very rarely sold out of season, as preserving was extremely difficult, although dried fruits like sultanas and raisins were quite often available.

Most Romano-British families were very fond of fish. They bought it fresh, if they lived near the sea or a river, or dried and salted otherwise. They also ate a considerable amount of shell-fish, particularly oysters, if they lived in the parts of the country where it was possible to obtain them.

Meat was not eaten as much as it is today. Nevertheless, every town had its butchers' shops, selling beef, mutton and pork, as well as chickens and ducks. Turkey was unknown, but there were a number of other delicacies to take its place, such as venison, wild boar, and sometimes even hedgehogs and dormice!

34 A market in the forum

◀ 35 Food and other goods were shipped from one country in the Roman Empire to another. Here a Roman officer supervises shipment of food and goods

Preparing the food

In the better-off homes all the food was prepared by slaves. Preparing usually meant smothering everything in a rich assortment of herbs, spices, nuts, honey and wine. Part of the reason for treating the food this way was that most people liked strong flavours, but also it disguised the fact that the food was not always as fresh as it should have been!

If the food needed to be cooked, it was nearly always boiled or fried. Baking and roasting were not entirely unknown, but they were rather difficult in the average Romano-British kitchen. For this, a small brick oven had to be built on the hearth, and a fire lit inside it. After the fire had burnt out, the ashes were raked away, the food was put inside the oven and the door shut very tightly.

Mealtimes

Most Romano-British families had three meals a day. The times of the meals varied considerably according to the season of the year. Breakfast was eaten as soon as it became light, dinner was between midday and four o'clock, and the evening meal, as far as possible, was eaten before it became dark.

▲
36 A lady serves in this greengrocer's shop

37 A pork butcher and his wife
▼

Breakfast in the average Romano-British family was a simple meal, usually consisting of some small round loaves made of wheat, with a cup of watered wine. Sometimes the children might have some honey on their bread (honey was the only form of sweetening known in Roman times), or perhaps an apple or a pear.

The next meal of the day was also a light one. Children sometimes came home from school for it, but they more often took a picnic lunch with them. There was usually a little cold meat or dried fish, some salad and bread, perhaps some fruit and some more watered wine.

The main meal of the day was taken in the evening. By this time the whole family had come home from work, had had their baths and were ready to relax. Before the meal could begin, however, the head of the family always made the customary offering of some little cakes and some wine to the household gods, and also said the traditional prayers. For most people the main meal consisted of a kind of savoury porridge, followed by some fruit and nuts, or perhaps some cheese. In winter there might be some hot wine. The children normally ate exactly the same food as the adults, and even quite a tiny child would be given a beaker filled with the same mixture of water and wine as the grown-ups were drinking.

When visitors came the evening meal was naturally much more elaborate. It might begin with a few shell-fish, some

38 A reconstruction of a Roman kitchen

39 Cooking implements: saucepan, ladle, painted plate and cake pan ▶

hard-boiled eggs or perhaps a dish of olives. Then the main part of the meal would be served, which might be several courses, each based on a different kind of meat or fish. Finally there would be fruit and nuts, or perhaps some kind of cakes and pastry. There was unlimited wine for everybody, including the children. Even when there were guests, however, people still picked up food with their fingers, as there were no forks in Roman Britain, only various types of knives and spoons.

40 Slaves serve a Roman meal. You can see that the man on the right is reclining on the couch to eat

After dinner in a rich man's house there might be some entertainment. This included acrobats, jugglers, dancers, singers and musicians. The music was usually provided by some stringed instruments, such as a lyre or a cithara, or by a cornu, an extremely long, thin trumpet, bent into one enormous circle.

41 Mosaic showing musicians (including two with cornus) and gladiators

7 Clothes

Children's clothes in Roman Britain were quite simple. In general, wool and flax were the only materials available, even to the richest Romano-British family. Cotton was known, but it was used chiefly for making the sails for ships, and silk, which was extremely costly, did not appeal to Roman taste. Furthermore, even the simplest garment took many hours to make. The wool or flax had to be first spun and then woven by hand into a rectangular or semicircular piece of cloth. This had to be taken to the fuller's to be cleaned (unless it was only to be worn by a slave) and bleached.

42 Shopkeepers examine cloth

43 Different lengths of tunic for male and female

Then it was combed and brushed, and finally sewn into the required shape and pressed.

If clothes were to be coloured, the wool or flax was dyed before the cloth was woven. Although the Romans had only natural dyes, they could produce almost all the colours that we have today. Their dyers used chiefly berries, leaves and roots, but the purple dye, famous because it was used for the purple worn by Roman emperors, was obtained from a sea-snail called the murex.

The basic garment worn by almost everyone in Roman Britain was a tunic. This was a straight, tube-like shift, either sleeveless or with sleeves down to the elbows. The boys' tunics reached to only a little below the knees, but the girls' tunics almost touched the ground and, in the case of better-off girls, were gracefully pleated.

Over their tunic most well-off boys wore a long toga. This was a kind of semi-circular wrap, that had to be wound round the body in a rather complicated way. Originally, only Roman citizens were allowed to wear a toga, but as time went on nearly all the better-off Romano-British families adopted the fashion. Well-off girls wore a similar long garment called a mantle. It was made of a rectangular piece of material which they wound round themselves in much the same way as a toga. Both togas and mantles were sometimes kept in place on the shoulders with large brooches, but many boys simply wore a belt round their tunics, and girls often did not bother about any kind of fastening at all.

44 In a cloth-merchant's shop. The men on the right are showing cloth for a toga. In the centre is a slave, dressed in a tunic. The two men seated on the left are wearing tunics and togas and the man standing is wearing a tunic and a hooded cloak

Under their tunic children wore either pants or a loin-cloth. In cold weather they occasionally wore a vest, but more often just two or three tunics, one on top of the other. There were no special nightshirts or nightdresses. Even the richest children went to bed in the same tunic that they had worn during the day.

In winter children wore thick woollen cloaks when they went out. They also changed their soft leather indoor sandals for strong hobnailed shoes. Even rich children never wore hats, but older girls sometimes covered their heads with their mantles, and the children's winter cloaks nearly always had hoods attached to them.

The tunics and togas of well-to-do boys were always white, although they sometimes had a narrow band of purple running from the shoulders to the hem. Boys could wear these tunics only until they were 14 or 15, however, because for a man to wear a tunic with a purple stripe was a sign that he held an official position. Girls also dressed in white in the early Romano-British period, but as time went on they began to wear tunics and mantles in attractive soft pastel shades. They never wore gaudy colours, however, except at their wedding, when the colours they were allowed to wear were very strictly laid down by tradition.

The outdoor cloaks, on the other hand, were often dyed quite dark colours. In fact, in later days dark red and green checks

45 A selection of Roman footwear

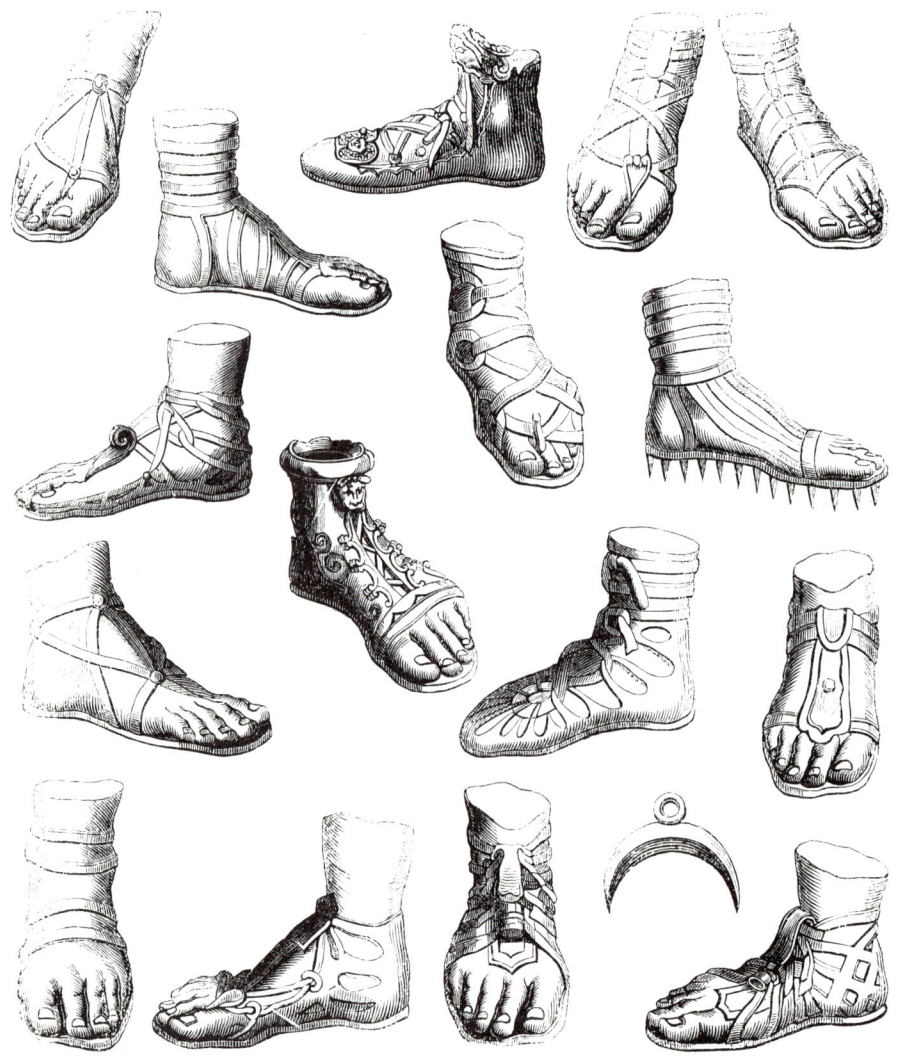

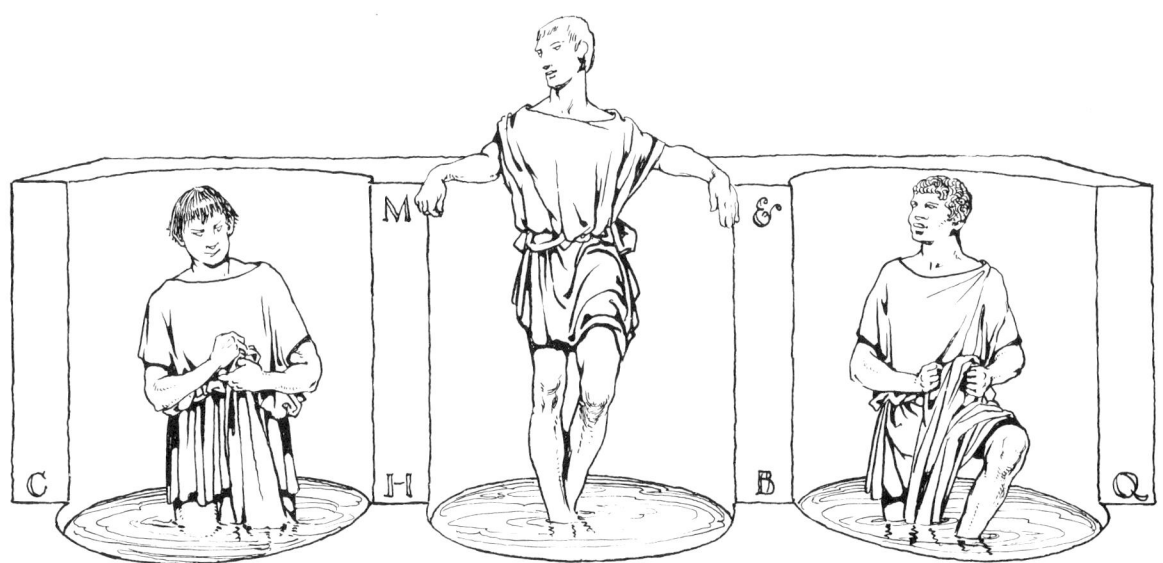

46 Fullers

became very popular. Presumably, in bad weather, when the streets were wet and muddy, it was impracticable, even for well-to-do children, to go out dressed entirely in white and pale colours.

Most better-off families sent their dirty clothes to the fuller's. There all the dirt was trodden out of them by bare-footed slaves in large vats of warm water. There was no soap, but fuller's earth was used instead. After the clothes had been washed, they were rinsed and carefully hung out to dry.

In general, there was little difference between children's and adults' dress. Boys' tunics were 10 to 20 centimetres shorter than mens' and sometimes had a stripe, but that was the only obvious distinction. Nevertheless, when a well-to-do boy came of age, at about 14, the setting aside of all the clothes he had worn as a child had a very important place in the celebrations. First the boy ceremoniously laid all his old clothes on the altar in front of the household gods, together with all his toys, games and other childish treasures. (These were later removed and either used by other members of the family or given to slaves.) Then he made an offering of the lucky charm which he had worn round his neck to ward off evil influences ever since he was nine days old.

Slaves' clothing

The children's old, discarded clothes were sometimes given to child slaves, but cloth was so expensive that usually even the rich used their worn-out clothing to make such things as blankets and saddle-cloths. In any case, the slaves could not have worn the togas or the mantles, as at no period in Roman Britain were these garments ever allowed to be worn by really low-born people.

Like everyone else, all young slaves and other poor children wore tunics. These were usually made of coarse fibres which had not been properly washed to get rid of the natural dirt and grease. Under their tunic they sometimes wore baggy trousers which reached down their legs and were tied round their ankles with rough leather thongs. When they went out poor children generally tied a piece of cloth round their shoulders, but in the winter they also wore capes of some very thick, coarse material. In fact, the capes were sometimes of leather, so that the slaves could work out of doors in the fields, or generally go about their master's business, whatever the weather.

8 Religion

The Celtic Church

When the Romans arrived in Britain they found people following the old Celtic religion. This was based on the belief that the whole of nature was filled with mysterious spirits and gods. The priests were known as druids, and most of the religious ceremonies and rites were held in the woods, especially in places where oak-trees and mistletoe were growing. The Romans were normally quite a tolerant people, and so at first they allowed the Celtic Church to continue in Britain alongside their own religious beliefs. They even allowed the

47 An Arch-druid

48 The Romans at first allowed the Celtic Church to build temples in Britain, modelled on ones like this, the Temple of Diana at Ephesus

druids to build temples, modelled on the great temples of Greece and Rome, with an inner sanctuary surrounded by rows of tall pillars. After a time, however, the Romans began to distrust the druids. They thought they were inciting some of the Britons to rebel against the Roman conquerors and, as a result, most of the druids were put to death. However, the Romans then incorporated many of the beliefs of the Celtic Church into their own religious faith.

The Roman religion

The Roman religion was observed in two ways, in public and in private. People attended public rites and observances in the towns; other customs and rituals went on in the home. From the children's point of view, it was obviously the domestic customs that were by far the more important, especially if they lived in out-of-the-way places and did not often visit any of the larger towns.

Domestic rites

The domestic rites centered around the house-gods, the Lares. In even the poorest homes there was always a statue of the Lares in the principle room, with a lamp burning in front of it (see picture 17). The Romans believed that the Lares would protect their homes from evil, and so from the time they

49 A sacrifice to the Lares

50 Statue of Mercury

were quite small the children were always taught to treat the gods with the greatest reverence and respect. In better-off homes several other gods were usually worshipped. The most important were Vesta, who looked after the fire and the hearth, and the Penates, who guarded the store-cupboards. There was also the two-headed god Janus, whose statue stood by the door, and who kept watch over everyone who went in and out of the house.

The father in each family acted as the priest for the rituals in the home. He gathered the rest of the household together at least once a day, and offered special prayers to the household gods. Also, at the main meal of the day some tiny cakes and a glass of wine were placed on the altar to the Lares, and a few pinches of salt were sprinkled on the lamp in front of their statue, which made it burn with a clear blue flame.

If the family owned some land they also worshipped the various gods of the fields. They always sacrificed the first fruits of the harvest to the gods and on feast-days killed an ox, pig or sheep in the gods' honour. Just as in the home, these rituals surrounding the prayers and sacrifices had to be correct in every detail, and performed at exactly the right moment, as laid down in the sacred law.

Public rites

The public religious rites centred around the great Roman deities. In early Roman Britain, the most important were Jupiter, Mars, Apollo, Mercury, Juno and Venus. The Roman emperor was also considered to be divine, and temples were dedicated to the emperor in most of the larger towns, although emperor worship was never very popular in Britain. From time to time various other gods were introduced to this country, mostly by soldiers who had served

51 The god Mithras

in the Middle East, and these were worshipped alongside the older gods. One of them was Isis, an Egyptian goddess who was supposed to look after the crops, and another was Serapis, a god of healing who was supposed to show you your future in your dreams, and who was also worshipped originally in Egypt.

52 A ceremony in a temple to Mithras

53 The remains of a Roman temple. You can see its simple, oblong shape and imagine the statue of the god at the far end

Many of the wealthier people also worshipped a god called Mithras. The worship of Mithras was probably brought to Britain from Persia by officers in the Roman legions who had served there. Mithras was regarded as the judge of the after-world, and it was he who decided whether people should go to heaven or to hell when they died. The temples to Mithras were always dark, mysterious places. In fact, one of the main attractions of the religion was probably that it was a kind of secret society. For instance, people were not allowed to enter the temples until they had passed various initiation rites, such as allowing themselves to be locked up for several hours all alone in a pitch-dark coffin.

Temples

All the gods and goddesses naturally had their own temples. These usually consisted of one long room only, with a statue of the god under an arched roof at one end. There was no special day of the week when Romano-British people went to the temples. They visited them whenever they wanted to ask for some special favour or give thanks for a favour received. Even the children went to the temples when they had some special reason for praying. Like the adults, they would first burn some incense, and then stand with their palms upturned in the Roman attitude of prayer. If they wanted to speak to a god or goddess they went as close as possible to the statue, and whispered in the god's ear, and then they would very reverently kiss the god's feet.

54 A Roman priest

Christianity

From the end of the first century AD a new religion began to appear in Britain. It was called Christianity, and it was brought mostly by soldiers and other travellers from Rome. It quickly spread all over Britain, particularly among the poorer sections of society, who were naturally attracted by Christ's promises of rewards in heaven for those who loved and served him faithfully on earth.

By the time Christianity arrived in Britain it was already viewed with suspicion by the Romans. People who were known to be Christians found that they were not being given posts of responsibility in the army and so on. As a result, the Christians in Britain had to use all kinds of secret codes, signs and passwords to avoid being detected. It was not until 250 AD, however, that a succession of emperors began systematic persecutions of the Christians all over the Empire, and countless men, women and children suddenly found themselves in danger. It was in one of these cruel and vicious purges that St. Alban was put to death. And yet, rather remarkably, the number of Christians in Britain continued to grow. In 313 AD an Act of Toleration was passed, and towards the end of the fourth century Christianity was established as the state religion throughout the whole Roman Empire.

55 A Christian schoolmaster who was beaten to death by his pupils for refusing to sacrifice to idols

9 Games and Pastimes

Romano-British children played many games which are still played today: for instance, hide-and-seek, leapfrog, tag and hop-scotch were all very popular. So was blind-man's buff, although it was played rather differently from the way it is nowadays. The children used to dance round the "blind man", tapping him with a stick, and shouting, "Come on and catch me!"

Small children also liked to play what was called the "jar game". One child sat on the ground while the other players came up in turn and pinched him and tweaked him. The child on the ground was not allowed to get up, but if he could grab hold of one of the other children while they were teasing him, the child he had caught had to take his place in the "jar".

Toys

There were all kinds of balls that small children could use for their games. A bouncy one was made out of a long length of wool wound tightly round a smooth stone. Small boys had kites, building bricks, hoops, tops and toy chariots, and both boys and girls liked to play on a see-saw or a swing. Little girls had dolls with jointed arms and legs. They probably had tiny dresses for them as well, but we cannot be sure, as these would all have rotted away long ago. Most of the toys were home-made, although a few, like the pottery rattles in the shape of animals, with pebbles inside them, were probably made by local craftsmen.

56 The tombstone of a young girl shows her with a pet cock and a kitten in her arms

▲
57 Hare-hunting mosaic

58 Dog modelled in bronze
▼

Sports

The most popular sport for older boys was, undoubtedly, hunting. The boys generally used bows and arrows, and hunted either on horseback or on foot. They also used hunting dogs. In fact, the British hunting dogs were so highly prized throughout the whole of the Roman world that they provided one of the country's chief

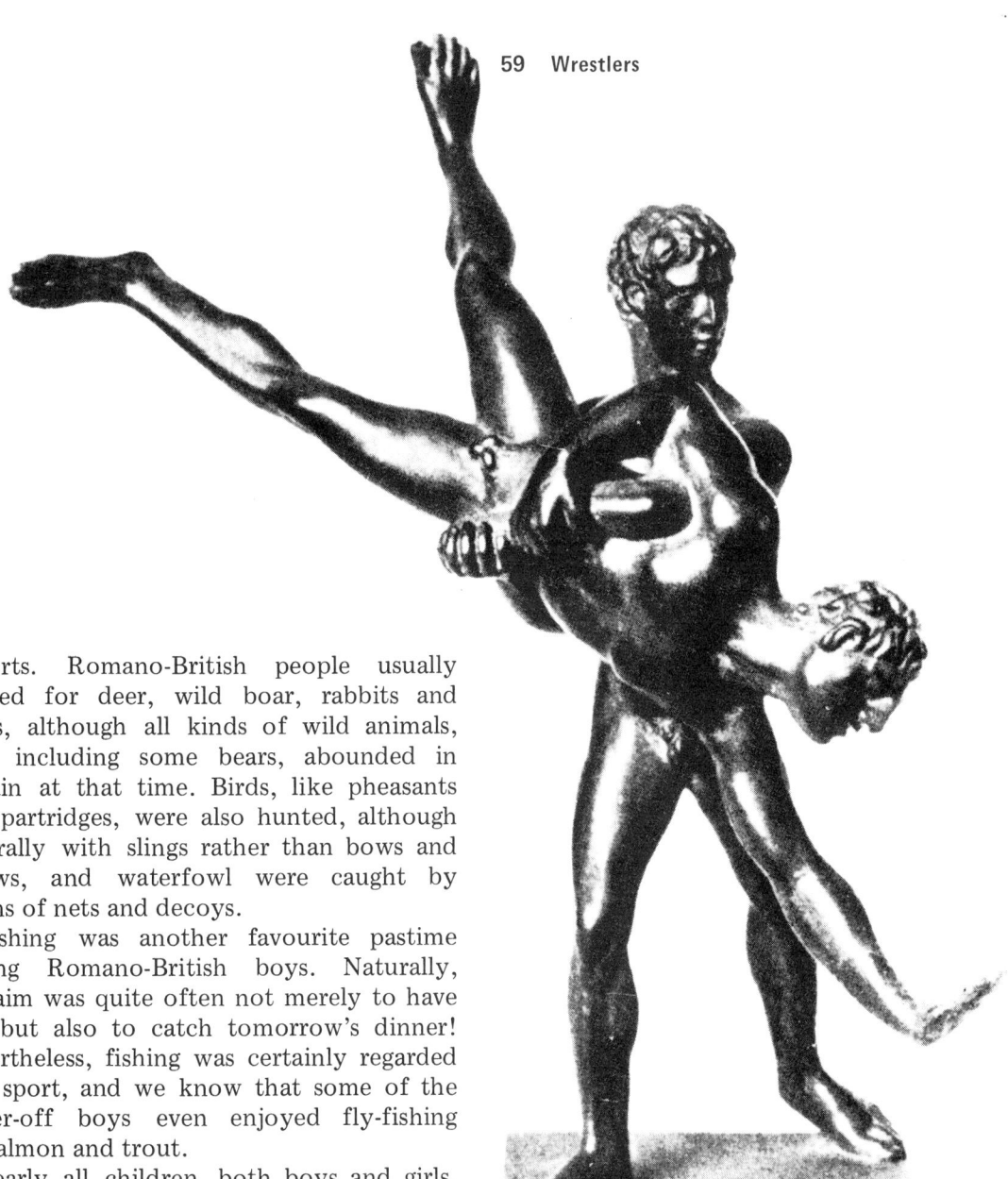

59 Wrestlers

exports. Romano-British people usually hunted for deer, wild boar, rabbits and hares, although all kinds of wild animals, even including some bears, abounded in Britain at that time. Birds, like pheasants and partridges, were also hunted, although generally with slings rather than bows and arrows, and waterfowl were caught by means of nets and decoys.

Fishing was another favourite pastime among Romano-British boys. Naturally, the aim was quite often not merely to have fun but also to catch tomorrow's dinner! Nevertheless, fishing was certainly regarded as a sport, and we know that some of the better-off boys even enjoyed fly-fishing for salmon and trout.

Nearly all children, both boys and girls, learnt to swim. Practically all the swimming took place either in the sea or in rivers and lakes, as only a few of the largest towns had a swimming-pool attached to the public baths. There were no swimming races or competitions like those we have today.

There were quite a number of popular ball games for older boys. One of them, called trigon, was a game for three players, and was played with a small solid ball. Each boy stood at the point of a large triangle, and they took turns at throwing the ball to each other, in rather the same way as the ball is thrown in present-day volley-ball. A gentler game was played

with a blown-up pig's bladder. Like trigon, it was played by three boys who stood at the points of a large triangle. In this game, though, the aim was to keep the ball in the air by kicking and heading it. In fact, the boys could use any part of their bodies except their hands to hit the ball.

Games were usually played in the fields or in the streets, but in some towns there was a special area in the public baths where various games could be played. In particular, games with a large leather ball filled with feathers were often played in these special excercise yards either before or after the boys went into the baths.

Older boys also took part in all kinds of athletics. Wrestling and boxing (which often took place in the exercise yards in the baths) were among the most popular, but running, jumping, discus throwing and even chariot racing were all enjoyed by the better-off Romano-British youths.

Indoor games

The most popular indoor pastimes in Roman Britain were probably board games. There were some that seem to have been like Ludo or Backgammon, and others that rather resembled Draughts or Chess. The boards were usually made of stone, but the counters might be pottery, wood or bone, and of any size and shape, from triangular to round. For the games resembling Ludo and Backgammon the children also needed dice. These had several different arrangements of dots; some were exactly like the dice we use today. The children generally just threw the dice down, two or three at a time, but occasionally they shook them first in some kind of dice cup.

There were no marbles in Roman Britain, but nuts took their place. In one game the children tried to throw the nuts into a narrow-necked vase. In another, four nuts were arranged in a pyramid, and the first

60   **A charioteer**

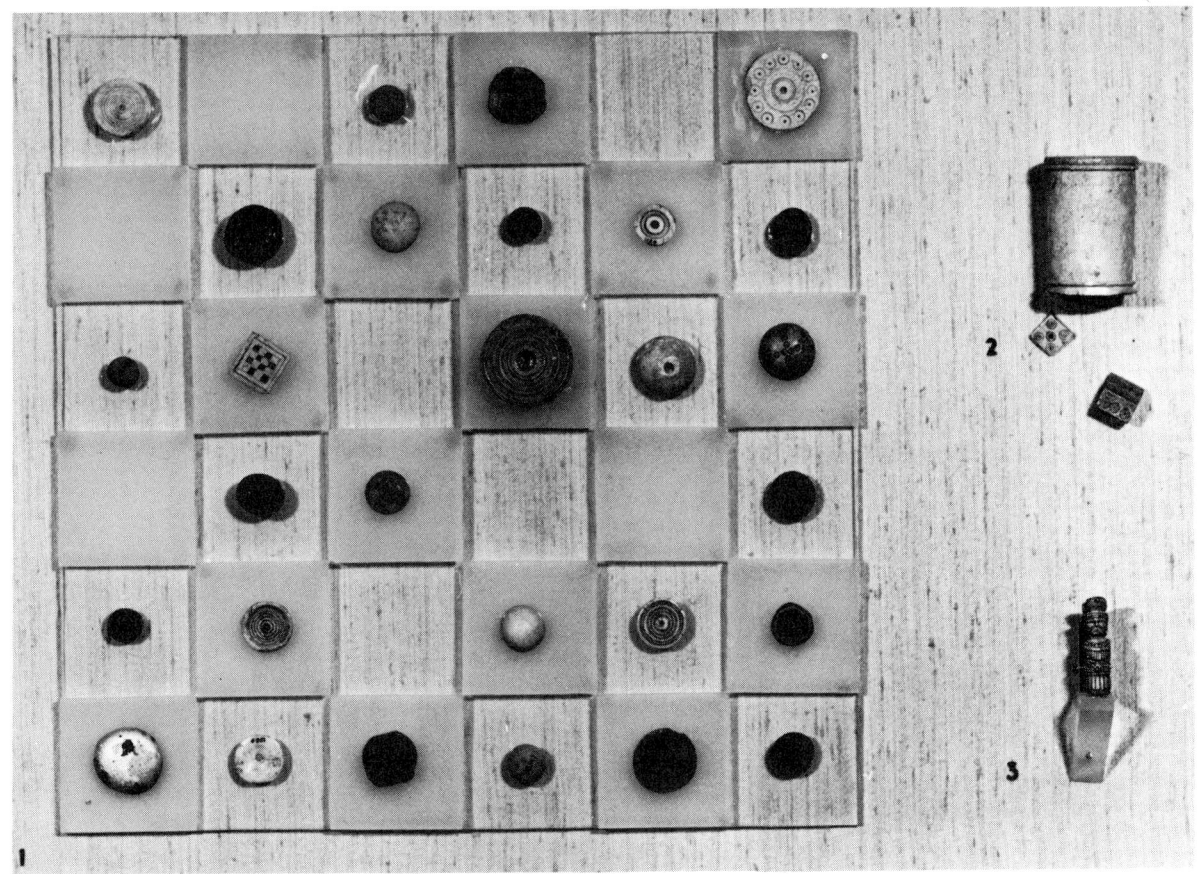

child who could knock the pyramid down with a fruit-stone or a pebble was given the nuts as a prize.

A very popular game among girls was known as Knucklebones. It was originally played with the small bones of sheep and goats, but later with bone-shaped pieces of metal or ivory. The game was almost exactly the same as the present-day Five-stones. The girls threw the bones up in the air and tried to catch them on the back of their hands.

61 A board game

Gambling

Romano-British people were very fond of gambling. Even quite small children often placed bets and wagers on who would win whatever game they were playing. In fact, children would often amuse themselves by placing bets on whether their friends had an odd or even number of pebbles or nuts hidden inside their clenched fists.

10 Poor Children

Before the Romans came to Britain most poor country people lived on the tops of the hills. This was partly because they thought they would be safe from their enemies on the higher ground, but a much more important reason was that the stronger, more important tribes, such as the Belgae, had gained control of most of the valleys, where the soil was more fertile and much easier to farm.

The homes of the poor country people were mostly small, isolated hovels. They lived almost entirely on what they could grow, and often had barely enough food to feed themselves. Occasionally, though, they had a better harvest than usual, and then they would come down from the hills and exchange their surplus produce for such things as salt, or perhaps some new farm implements.

The children of these poor families were lucky if they even survived infancy. The majority of them died either from malnutrition or from lack of any proper medical care while they were still babies. Those children who did grow up, however, almost invariably continued to live in the same simple, hand-to-mouth fashion as their parents and grandparents had done before them.

When the Romans arrived the way of life of most of these poor families hardly altered. The Romans usually did not even bother to collect tax from them, as they lived in such out-of-the-way places. In fact, even the poor people who were living in the settled, Romanized part of the country were probably hardly aware that their land had been conquered.

These poor country-dwellers were by no means the only poor people in Roman Britain, however. Countless desperately poor families lived in squalor in every large town and city. There was little that most of these poor families could do except beg, although the better-off Romano-British people generally despised the poor and had little sympathy with them.

Child slaves

Sometimes the poor people were so desperate that they sold their children as slaves. (In Roman times every father had the right

◀ 62   A Roman village

63   A child's coffin, made of lead ▶

64 Slaves on a farm would have to work a plough. This is a bronze model of a Romano-British plough

to sell his children if he wished.) The money received for a child would have bought a few necessities for the rest of the family, and some parents may even have thought that the child would have a better life as a slave than they could have given him themselves.

There were various other ways in which children became slaves. They were sometimes kidnapped (like the future St. Patrick) and put on sale in the slave market. Although it was strictly against the law to sell a free-born child into slavery, once the child had been carried off and sold it was virtually impossible to trace him and free him. Other children became slaves when their fathers fell into debt. This usually happened in the case of the children of small shopkeepers and craftsmen. According to Roman law, if a person could not pay his debts he became the property of his creditor, and in most cases his wife and children generally became the slaves of the creditor, too.

By far the greatest proportion of child slaves were the children of slave parents, however. Every child born to a slave was the property of the mother's master from the moment of birth. (The fathers had no right over the children because the slave women were not officially allowed to marry.) If the master needed some more slaves he would probably keep the baby; otherwise he might well sell the child to some other wealthy slave-owner. This separation of parents and children was one of the worst aspects of slavery. In fact, even the Romans, who were not usually kind or compassionate, eventually came to realize this, and in later Roman Britain it became the law that husbands, wives and small children, who were all slaves, could only be sold together, as a family.

Officially, the slaves were the poorest people of all in Roman Britain. They could not legally own anything, not even the clothes and the shoes they stood up in.

62

In practice, however, slaves were not too badly off, for if a man had paid a good price for a slave, he usually tried to make sure that the slave was well fed and well clothed and kept reasonably contented.

The price of a slave could vary quite considerably. On average, a well-trained, well-educated slave cost at least ten times as much as an untrained slave. Wealthy people sometimes took a special fancy to a particular slave they saw for sale, though, especially an attractive looking child, and they would then be willing to pay almost any price the slave-trader asked.

Slaves were employed for all kinds of jobs. In a well-to-do home, for instance, they might work in the kitchen, the laundry, the stables or the garden. The lady of the house always had her own personal slaves to do her hair and make her clothes, and slaves were also employed as nurse-maids for the children. On a large estate there might be two or three hundred slaves. Most of them were employed either to till the ground or to look after the animals. There were always a certain number of artisans, though, such as blacksmiths and bricklayers, and if a young slave showed any special aptitude, he was usually apprenticed to one of these trades.

65 Mosaic of agricultural scenes

Really intelligent young slaves were even sent to school and college, and could then become doctors and teachers. In fact, nearly all doctors and teachers were slaves. It was naturally expensive for a slave-owner to educate a boy in this way, but he could always get his money back, if he wished, by selling the slave when his education was finished.

All the food and clothes for the slaves were provided, of course, by the slave-owner. Some better-off Romano-British people also gave their slaves regular pocket money. The slaves could either spend this on any small luxuries they wanted, or else save it until at last they had acquired enough money to buy their freedom. Other slaves were rewarded with their freedom if they performed some outstanding service for their master. Yet others were given their freedom on the death of the man for whom they had worked. Whatever the reason for which they were freed, the former slaves and all their descendants became officially freed-men, with all the rights and duties of Romano-British citizens.

Table of Major Events in Roman Britain and Elsewhere in the Roman Empire

		BRITAIN	ELSEWHERE IN THE ROMAN EMPIRE
BC	753		Rome was founded by Romulus.
	58		Julius Caesar began his conquest of Gaul.
	55	Julius Caesar's first invasion of Britain.	
	54	Julius Caesar's second invasion.	
	44		Julius Caesar assassinated.
	27		Augustus Caesar became Emperor.
AD	29		Crucifixion of Jesus.
	43	Claudius Caesar invaded Britain.	
	51	The British chief, Caractacus was taken prisoner by the Romans.	
	61	Queen Boudicca led the Iceni in revolt against the Romans, but was defeated and killed herself.	
	64		Great fire of Rome.
	78	Julius Agricola arrived in Britain.	
	79		Pompeii destroyed by a volcanic eruption.
	117		Hadrian became Emperor.
	121	Hadrian visited Britain, and ordered a defensive wall to be built.	
	150	By this time Romano-British life was well established.	
	196	Northern British tribes overran Hadrian's Wall, but the Romans recaptured and repaired it.	
	250	Saxon raids began on south-east England.	
	285	Forts were built along most of the east and south-east coast.	
	312		Constantine became Emperor.
	313		The Edict of Toleration allowed Christians to worship freely in all parts of the Empire.

364	Hadrian's Wall was severely damaged by the Picts from Scotland.	
385	Hadrian's Wall was abandoned, and most of the Roman troops left Britain.	The Romans were defeated in battle in northern Italy.
394		Christianity was established as the official religion throughout the Empire.
410	The British appealed to Rome to send reinforcements to defend them against the Saxons.	Rome captured by the Visigoths.
429	The last of the Romans left, and the British made their last appeal for help.	
455		Rome sacked by the Vandals.
476		The Roman Empire came to an end.

Glossary

abacus — a counting frame with beads which are moved along a number of parallel wires

basilica — a large oblong hall, usually with a double row of pillars at the front, and a semi-circular arch at the far end, used for judicial and other business

Belgae — an ancient British tribe who originated in Belgium

Belgic — belonging to the Belgae

Celtic — the language of the Celts, the ancient inhabitants of Cornwall, Wales and various other parts of Britain; also means belonging to the Celts

druids — priests of the ancient Celtic tribes, who worshipped under oak-trees

flax — the fibres of a purple-flowered plant, used for making linen

forum — a market place, where legal as well as commercial business was carried on

fullers — bleachers or cleaners of cloth

fuller's earth — a soft clay, which absorbs grease, used for bleaching or cleaning cloth

hypocaust — an underground chamber, containing a fire, which diffused its heat by a system of flues to rooms or baths above it

mosaic — inlaid work, in which the designs are formed by small pieces of coloured marble, fixed on a ground of stucco to make a flooring

murex — a kind of sea-snail exuding a yellow fluid which turns purple when exposed to light and from which purple dye was obtained

papyrus — a kind of reed, the pith of which was used in ancient times for making paper

province — a portion of an empire, usually having its own governor

strigil — a sickle-shaped instrument for toning up the skin after a bath

stylus — a pen, especially for scratching on wax

toga — the loose outer garment worn by Roman citizens

venison — the flesh of the deer

villa — a country house

A Selection of Sites in Roman Britain

	Roman name
Anglesey	Mona
Bath (Avon)	Aquae Suli
Bradwell (Essex)	Othona
Buxton (Derbyshire)	Aquae Arnemetiae
Caerleon (Gwent)	Isca Silurum
Caister (Norfolk)	Venta Icenorum
Canterbury (Kent)	Durovernum Cantiacorum
Carlisle (Cumbria)	Luguvallium
Chester (Cheshire)	Deva
Chesters (Northumberland)	Cilurnum
Chichester (West Sussex)	Noviomagus Regnensium
Cirencester (Glos.)	Corinium Dubunnorum
Colchester (Essex)	Camulodunum
Dover (Kent)	Dubris
Exeter (Devon)	Isca Dumnoniorum
Gloucester (Glos.)	Glevum
Housesteads (Northumberland)	Vercovicium
Isle of Wight	Vectis
Leicester (Leics.)	Ratae Coritanorum
Lincoln (Lincs.)	Lindum
London	Londinium
Pevensey (East Sussex)	Anerita
Rochester (Kent)	Durobrivae
St. Albans (Herts.)	Verulamium
Silchester (Hampshire)	Calleva Atrebatum
Winchester (Hampshire)	Venta Belgarum
Wroxeter (Salop)	Viroconium
York (North Yorks.)	Eburacum

Places to Visit

BATH, Avon	Roman baths, the most complete remains in Britain. Also a museum.
BIGNOR, West Sussex	Roman villa, with fine mosaic pavements. Also a museum.
BRADING, Isle of Wight	Roman villa, with mosaic pavements and hypocaust.
CAERLEON, Gwent	Legionary fortress, with amphitheatre that could accommodate six thousand people. Also a museum.
CAERNARFON, Gwynedd	Roman fort and museum.
CHEDWORTH, Glos.	One of the best preserved Roman villas in Britain, with mosaics and hypocausts.
CHESTER, Cheshire	One of the finest museums of Roman remains in the country.
CIRENCESTER, Glos.	Museum containing mosaic floors, Romano-British sculpture and many items of everyday Romano-British life.
COLCHESTER, Essex	Roman gateway. Also a museum.
CORBRIDGE, Northumberland	Remains of a Roman fort, including granaries. Also a museum.
DOVER, Kent	Roman lighthouse. Also remains of a large Roman town house, with the best-preserved Roman wall paintings in Britain.
FISHBOURNE, West Sussex	The largest Roman palace in Britain, with many mosaic pavements.
GREAT YARMOUTH, Norfolk	Burgh Castle, a massive third-century Roman shore fort.
HOUSESTEADS, Northumberland	Roman fort and five-kilometre stretch of Hadrian's Wall.
LONDON	The Temple of Mithras, near the Mansion House. Also Roman exhibits in the Guildhall Museum and the British Museum.
LULLINGSTONE, Kent	Roman villa.
ST. ALBANS, Herts.	Roman theatre and hypocaust. Also a museum.
SILCHESTER, Hampshire	Remains of a Roman town. Also a museum.
WALWICK, Northumberland	Chesters Roman fort, built to garrison five hundred cavalry soldiers, with a fine bath house. Remains of a Roman bridge nearby. Also a museum.
WROXETER, Salop	Remains of a Roman town, including baths and colonnade.
YORK, North Yorks.	Remains of Roman town walls and a stretch of Roman road. Also a museum containing some Roman toys.

Books for Further Reading

Non-fiction

Allen, Kenneth, *One Day in Roman Britain* (Tyndall)
Birley, Anthony, *Life in Roman Britain* (Batsford)
Burrell, R.E.C., *The Romans in Britain* (Wheaton)
Cottrell, Leonard, *Seeing Roman Britain* (Evans)
Priestley, Harold, *Britain under the Romans* (Warne)
Priestley, Harold, *The Observer's Book of Ancient and Roman Britain* (Warne)
Quennell, M. & C., *Everyday Life in Roman Britain* (Batsford)
Richmond, I., *Roman Britain* (Penguin)
Seliman, R.R., *Roman Britain* (Methuen)
Thwaite, Anthony, *Beyond the Inhabited World* (Andre Deutsch)

Fiction

Chapman, Vera, *Judy and Julia* (Rex Collings)
Finkel, George, *Twilight Province* (Angus and Robertson)

Index

The numbers in **bold type** refer to the figure numbers of the illustrations

abacus, 11
acrobats, 42
agriculture, 35
Apollo, 51
appeals to Rome, 10
arenas, 28
artisans, 26

ball games, 55, 57-8
bands, 28
barbarians, 10
basilicas, 24
bear-baiting, 28
Belgae, 5, 60
board games, 58; **61**
boxing, 58
brick-works, 35
brides, 19-22
British tribes, 5
brooches, 45
butchers' shops, 36; **37**

candles, 35
canings, 17
carpenters, 26
Celtic language, 11
chariot races, 28, 58; **60**
chests, 31, 35; **31**
Christianity, 18, 53-4; **55**
citharas, 42
classrooms, 11
Claudius, 5; **4**
cloaks, 46; **44**
coal, 31, 35
cock-fighting, 28
colours for clothes, 46-7
coming of age, 47
consecration of babies, 18

Constantine, 7
cooking, 18, 33, 39; **39**
cornus, 42
cosmetics, 20
cotton, 43
couches, 33, 35; **40**
craftsmen, 26, 55, 62; **7**
culture, 6
curling tongs, 20
customs, 6
cut-throats, 23
cymbals, 28

dancing, 18, 42
debates, 15
dice, 58
discipline, 17
discus throwing, 58
doctors, 22, 64
dogs, 56; **58**
dolls, 55
druids, 48, 50; **47**
dyes, 45

Egypt, 51
elementary education, 11, 17, 27
embroidery, 18
emperor worship, 51
entertainment, 42; **24**
estates, 27, 30, 35

farmers, 36; **64, 65**
feast days, 15, 28
festivals, 28
figures, 11; **10**
fish, 11
fishing, 57

flax, 43, 45
floggings, 17
forts, 5
forums, 24-5, 28, 36; **34**
fourth century, 10
France, 5
fruit, 36
fullers, 43, 47; **46**
furniture, 31; **32**

gambling, 59
gardens, 30
Gaul, 5
Gauls, 5
gigs, 22
girls' education, 18
gladiator fights, 28; **25, 41**
glass, 35
gods, 28, 48, 51, 53
government service, 15
grammar, 15
grammar schools, 15
Greece, 15
Greek literature, 18
Greeks, 27
Greek writers, 15

Hadrian, 11; **4**
hair styles, 20
honey, 40
household gods, 19, 40, 47, 50-1; **17**
housewives, 36
hunting, 56-7; **57**
hypocausts, 31; **30**

industry, 7
Isis, 51

Italy, 10

Janus, 51
jugglers, 42
Julius Agricola, 5
Julius Caesar, 5
Juno, 51
Jupiter, 51

kitchens, 33; **38**
knucklebones, 59

language, 6
Lares, 19, 40, 47, 50-1; **49**
Latin, 11
law courts, 15, 26
lawyers, 26
literature, 15
litters, 22
lucky charms, 18, 19, 47
lyres, 15, 18, 42; **14**

malnutrition, 61
mantles, 45-7; **43**
market places, 24
markets, 36; **34**
marriage, 19
Mars, 51
mathematics, 15
meals, 33, 39-40; **40**
merchants, 36
Mercury, 51; **50**
military zones, 5
Minerva, 15; **12**
Mithras, 53; **51, 52**
mosaics, 31; **7, 29, 57**
murex, 45
music, 15
musicians, 42; **24, 41**

night-clothes, 46

oil-lamps, 35
omens, 22
one-man businesses, 26
one-teacher schools, 15
ovens, 39
oysters, 36

pageants, 28
papyrus rolls, 11; **9**
Penates, 51
Persia, 53

philosophy, 15
pirates, 7
plays, 28; **24**
population, 7
potteries, 35
potters, 26
prayers, 28, 51, 53
priests, 22, 28; **54**
processions, 28
proverbs, 17
public baths, 28-9, 31, 57-8
public religious rites, 50-1
public speaking, 15

reclining at table, 33; **40**
religious ceremonies, 19, 28
robbers, 23
Roman citizens, 45
Roman Empire, 5
Roman invasion of Britain, 5; **1, 5**
Roman literature, 18
Roman Province of Britain, 5, 10
Roman withdrawal from Britain, 10; **6**
Romano-British way of life, 6
Rome, 5

sandals, 46; **45**
Saxons, 7, 10; **5**
school classes, 11
school day, 17
school holidays, 15
schools, 11, 27; **11**
school year, 15
science, 15
secondary schools, 15
Serapis, 15
shell-fish, 36, 40
shoes, 46; **45**
shopkeepers, 22, 24, 36, 62; **42**
shops, 11, 24, 26, 36; **22, 23, 36, 44**
singing, 15, 18, 42
slaves, 15, 19, 22-3, 27, 35-6, 39, 47, 61-4; **16**
slaves' quarters, 35
south of England, 5, 6
spinning, 18
stoves, 33
street lighting, 23

streets, 24
strigils, 29
stucco, 30
stylus, 11
swimming, 57

tambourines, 28
tanneries, 35
tanners, 26
tax relief, 11
teachers, 11, 15, 22, 64; **11**
temples, 28, 50-1, 53; **48, 52, 53**
tenant farmers, 35; **33**
theatres, 28
tiles, 30
tile-works, 35
tin, 5
togas, 45-7; **44**
toilets, 31
town-dwellers, 26-7
town walls, 24; **20, 21**
toys, 55
trade, 7
traders, 36
trigon, 57
trousers, 47
trumpets, 28, 42
tunics, 45-7; **43, 44**
tutors, 18

underfloor heating, 29, 31; **30**

vegetables, 36
Venus, 51
verandahs, 25, 30; **27**
Vesta, 51
villas, 30-1; **27, 28**

weavers, 26
weaving, 18
weddings, 19-22, 46; **18, 19**
wind instruments, 28; **15**
windows, 35
wine, 41
wool, 43, 45
workrooms, 26-7; **7**
wrestling, 58; **59**
writing tablets, 11; **8, 9**

yard-arm, 36; **37**